Brown Bears

written and photographed
by Lynn M. Stone

Lerner Publications Company • Minneapolis, Minnesota

For Melanie
   • —LMS

Thanks to our series consultant, Sharyn Fenwick, elementary science/math specialist. Mrs. Fenwick was the winner of the National Science Teachers Association 1991 Distinguished Teaching Award. She also was the recipient of the Presidential Award for Excellence in Math and Science Teaching, representing the state of Minnesota at the elementary level in 1992.

Additional photographs are reproduced through the courtesy of: pp. 27, 33, 35, © 1998 Leonard Lee Rue III; p. 29 © 1998 Rick McIntyre.

Early Bird Nature Books were conceptualized
by Ruth Berman and designed by Steve Foley.
Series editor is Joelle Goldman.

Website address: www.lernerbooks.com

Library of Congress Cataloging-in-Publication Data

Stone, Lynn M.
   Brown Bears / written and photographed by Lynn M. Stone.
      p.   cm.—(Early bird nature books)
   Includes index.
   Summary: Describes the physical characteristics and habits of the large bears that thrive on the southern coast of Alaska.
   ISBN 0-8225-3029-5 (alk. paper)
   1. Kodiak bear—Juvenile literature. [1. Kodiak bear. 2. Brown bear. 3. Bears.] I. Title. II. Series.
   QL737.C27S7285   1998
   599.784—dc21   97-38175

Manufactured in the United States of America
1 2 3 4 5 6 – SP – 03 02 01 00 99 98

Contents

RUSSIA

Alaska (U.S.)

Brown bears live in Europe, Asia, and North America. Some brown bears in Alaska are called brownies. The striped area shows where brownies live.

CANADA

N

Be a Word Detective

Can you find these words as you read about the brown bear's life? Be a detective and try to figure out what they mean. You can turn to the glossary on page 46 for help.

biologist   habitat   omnivores
carcasses   hibernates   predators
cubs   home range   sanctuary
den   litter

Chapter 1

This is a brown bear. How many kinds of bears are there?

Alaska's Big Bears

Do you know where the world's biggest fishermen live? They live in Alaska. They are not people. They are brown bears.

The world has eight species, or kinds, of bears. All species of bears are large and furry. All of them have stubby tails and paws with long, sharp claws.

These brown bears are not fighting. They are playing.

Brown bears are the world's biggest bears. Their fur is usually medium brown. Some brown bears have light brown fur. Others have fur that is almost black.

Brown bears live in wild parts of Europe, Asia, and North America. In North America, most brown bears are called "grizzly bears."

Brown bears see and smell well.

Brownies are found in southern Alaska. They live near the ocean.

Some brown bears live on Alaska's southern coast. Many of these bears live on the mainland, near the ocean. Others live on islands. These brown bears are often called "brownies." Sometimes they are called "big brown bears."

All brown bears have a hump on their shoulders.
The hump is made of fat and muscle.

Brownies are bigger than other brown bears. A male brownie may be nearly 10 feet tall when he stands on his back legs. He could almost bump his head on a basketball hoop. He may weigh more than 1,500 pounds. That is more than an entire class of second graders.

Brownies are strong animals. They are much bigger than adult humans.

Alaska has many wild areas. Brownies live in wild places like this one.

A habitat is a place where a kind of animal can live and grow. Alaska's southern coast has beaches, rivers, and streams. There are shrubby hills, meadows, and forests. There are mountains and valleys. These places are the habitat of Alaska's giant bears.

A brownie may travel many miles in one day. It may visit a beach, a forest, and a meadow along the way.

Chapter 2

This brownie is eating a kind of plant called sedge. What other foods do brownies eat?

Finding Food

Brownies are omnivores (AHM-nih-vorz). Omnivores eat both plants and animals. In spring, brownies eat mostly plants. They dig up roots. They eat grasses. They eat sedge. Sedge is a kind of plant that grows in meadows.

Brownies are also predators (PREH-duh-turz). Predators hunt and eat other animals. Brownies hunt ground squirrels and young moose.

A brownie might hunt and eat a ground squirrel like this one.

Some brownies hunt for clams on the seashore. Clams live in the sand. To find clams, brownies dig big holes in the sand. The holes are deep and round, like popcorn bowls. Clams have hard shells. When a brownie finds a clam, the bear uses its claws to open the shell. Then the bear licks out the clam.

A brownie is digging many holes in the sand. The bear is looking for clams.

A brownie uses its claws to open a clam's hard shell. Then the brownie licks the clam out of the shell.

Sometimes brownies eat carcasses. A carcass is the body of a dead animal. Brownies eat moose and deer carcasses. They eat whale and seal carcasses that have washed onto beaches.

As brownies look for food, they travel in a big area. This area is called a home range. The bears make miles of winding trails through their home range.

A brownie does not sleep all night. Instead, it takes many short naps during the night and day.

Sometimes many brownies use the same trail. The trail becomes well worn.

Brownies mostly stay away from each other. But many brownies may share a home range. A brownie's home range is huge. Brownies can share a home range and still stay apart.

Chapter 3

This brownie has caught a fish called a salmon. Do brownies catch many salmon?

Bear Fishing

In summer, brownies eat mostly salmon. Salmon are fish. They are born in rivers. But they spend most of their lives in the ocean. Each summer adult salmon leave the ocean. They swim into the rivers where they were born. They go upstream to lay their eggs. Thousands of salmon swim up Alaska's rivers each year.

*Sometimes a brownie catches more salmon than it
can eat in one day. Gulls eat the leftover salmon.
None of it is wasted.*

Brownies are good at catching fish. They
can catch 10 to 20 salmon in one day. People
saw one brownie catch 91 salmon in one day!

These brownies are fishing in shallow water. A brownie is using its big paws to grab a salmon.

Most brownies stand in shallow water to fish. When a salmon swims by, the bear pounces on it. The bear uses its big, rough paws to hold the fish down. Then the bear grabs the fish in its jaws.

Some bears fish by belly-flopping. They flop on their bellies into the water. Sometimes they land on a fish.

This bear is jumping into the water to catch a salmon.

Some brownies wait for salmon at the top of a waterfall.

Brownies have other ways of fishing, too.
Sometimes they fish at the top of a waterfall.
As salmon jump up the falls, the bears wait
with their jaws open. Sometimes a salmon
accidentally lands in a bear's mouth.

In some rivers, many brownies fish at the same time. Big bears sometimes steal salmon from smaller bears. But there are usually lots of salmon. Most often, the bears do not have to fight for fish.

These brownies are fighting over a salmon.

Salmon is a healthy food for bears.
Scientists think big brown bears are so big
because they eat so much salmon.

Salmon swim into a few rivers again in the fall.
Brownies who live near those rivers get to eat
more salmon.

Berries make a good meal for a brownie.

By late August, the salmon have laid their eggs. The fish die. Fall begins, and berries ripen. Big brown bears eat berries they find in meadows and on hillsides.

Chapter 4

Snow covers berries and other food in winter. Where do brown bears spend the winter?

Winter Bears

The bears have eaten well all summer and fall. They have a thick layer of fat under their skin. They are ready for winter.

By November, snow falls in Alaska. Food is hard to find. Brownies look for a place to spend the winter.

Brownies spend the winter in a den. A den is any place where a bear can stay snug. Some brownies dig burrows in hillsides. Some dig holes in deep snow. Others use a cave as a den.

A brown bear dug this den in a hillside.

Winter lasts for about six months in Alaska.

Outside, the world is cold. Being underground helps a brownie stay snug. A brownie's layer of fat helps to hold in its body's heat. The bear's thick fur keeps it warm.

In the den, a big brown bear hibernates (HYE-bur-nates). It enters a deep sleep. Its body slows down. Its heart beats more slowly. The bear breathes more slowly, too.

A brownie does not eat when it hibernates. It uses its body fat for food while it sleeps. The bear hibernates for five months or longer.

Most often, a brownie awakens in April. It has been a long time since the bear has eaten. It is very hungry. It begins to look for food.

At the end of winter, brownies are thin and hungry.

Chapter 5

Winter is when brown bears are born. Does a mother brownie awaken from her winter's sleep to take care of her babies?

Raising a Family

A female brownie has her babies in the winter den. Baby bears are called cubs. Cubs are usually born in January. The mother awakens just a little when she gives birth. Then she slips back into hibernation.

A mother brownie usually has two cubs at a time. She may have as many as six. A group of cubs is called a litter.

Newborn cubs are tiny. Each cub weighs less than 1 pound. Cubs are helpless. They are blind. They cannot walk. They have no fur.

This brown bear cub is about 10 days old.

Even though the cubs' mother is sleeping, she gives them everything they need. The cubs drink her milk. They stay warm by cuddling near her warm body.

In April, the mother bear wakes up. She leads the cubs outside.

Usually only two or three cubs in a litter live long enough to leave the den in April.

These cubs are drinking their mother's milk.

By April, the cubs are about four months old. Each weighs 10 to 12 pounds. The cubs can see and walk. They are furry and playful.

The mother bear raises her cubs alone.
The cubs' father does not help care for them.
Adult brown bears live apart from each other.

A brownie shows her cubs how to find food. These cubs are about six months old.

This brownie is protecting her cubs from a male bear.

The mother bear stays away from adult male bears. A male might attack and kill her cubs. A male bear is much larger and stronger than a female bear. But a mother bear will fight a male bear to defend her cubs.

The mother brownie and her cubs travel together all summer and fall. They hunt for food in their home range. They hibernate together in winter.

When the cubs are two or three years old, they can take care of themselves. Then the mother brownie chases the cubs away. She is ready to start a new family.

These cubs are waiting while their mother fishes. She will return with a salmon for them to eat.

Cubs sometimes stay together after they leave their mother. They may travel together for two or three more years. When young bears are about five or six years old, they are old enough to start their own families.

These bears are about three years old. Soon they will start families of their own.

Chapter 6

This is the McNeil River. Why do so many brownies come to the McNeil River each summer?

Watching Brownies

Alaska has a place where people can see many brownies at once. It is the McNeil River State Game Sanctuary. A sanctuary is a safe place. The McNeil River sanctuary is a safe place for brown bears. Hunters cannot shoot brownies there.

Each summer, many brown bears visit the McNeil River waterfall to catch salmon. A few people are allowed to visit the waterfall, too. The visitors hike to the waterfall with a biologist. A biologist is a scientist who studies living things. The McNeil River sanctuary is a great place to study brown bears.

More brown bears gather at the McNeil River waterfall than at any other place on earth.

At the waterfall, the visitors sit quietly. They watch the bears fish. They watch some of the bears belly-flop into a deep, blue pool. They hear the bears growl at each other. Sometimes visitors see as many as 75 brown bears at once.

This brown bear dived underwater to catch a salmon.

Maybe you will visit the McNeil River someday. Then you will see how brownies fish. And you will know how to fish like a bear!

The McNeil River State Game Sanctuary is a safe place for brownies to live.

On Sharing a Book

As you know, adults greatly influence a child's attitude toward reading. When a child sees you read, or when you share a book with a child, you're sending a message that reading is important. Show the child that reading a book together is important to you. Find a comfortable, quiet place. Turn off the television and limit other distractions like telephone calls.

Be prepared to start slowly. Take turns reading parts of this book. Stop and talk about what you're reading. Talk about the photographs. You may find that much of the shared time is spent discussing just a few pages. This discussion time is valuable for both of you, so don't move through the book too quickly. If the child begins to lose interest, stop reading. Continue sharing the book at another time. When you do pick up the book again, be sure to revisit the parts you have already read. Most importantly, enjoy the book!

Be a Vocabulary Detective

You will find a word list on page 5. Words selected for this list are important to the understanding of the topic of this book. Encourage the child to be a word detective and search for the words as you read the book together. Talk about what the words mean and how they are used in the sentence. Do any of these words have more than one meaning? You will find these words defined in a glossary on page 46.

What about Questions?

Use questions to make sure the child understands the information in this book. Here are some suggestions:

> What did this paragraph tell us? What does this picture show? What do you think we'll learn about next? Could a brown bear live in your backyard? Why/Why not? How do brownies get their food? Would you like to eat the things that brownies eat? How is a brownie family like your family and how is it different? What do you think it's like to spend the winter in a den? What is your favorite part of the book? Why?

If the child has questions, don't hesitate to respond with questions of your own like: What do *you* think? Why? What is it that you don't know? If the child can't remember certain facts, turn to the index.

Introducing the Index

The index is an important learning tool. It helps readers get information quickly without searching throughout the whole book. Turn to the index on page 48. Choose an entry, such as *claws,* and ask the child to use the index to find out how brownies use their claws. Repeat this exercise with as many entries as you like. Ask the child to point out the differences between an index and a glossary. (The index helps readers find information quickly, while the glossary tells readers what words mean.)

Where in the World?

Many plants and animals found in the Early Bird Nature Books series live in parts of the world other than the United States. Encourage the child to find the places mentioned in this book on a world map or globe. Take time to talk about climate, terrain, and how you might live in such places.

All the World in Metric!

Although our monetary system is in metric units (based on multiples of 10), the United States is one of the few countries in the world that does not use the metric system of measurement. Here are some conversion activities you and the child can do using a calculator:

WHEN YOU KNOW:	MULTIPLY BY:	TO FIND:
miles	1.609	kilometers
feet	0.3048	meters
inches	2.54	centimeters
gallons	3.787	liters
pounds	0.454	kilograms

Activities

Draw or color a picture of a brownie. Brownies visit meadows, forests, rivers, and ocean beaches. They travel in valleys and mountains. In winter, brownies stay in dens. Draw your picture with a brownie in the place you like best.

Pretend you're a biologist. Plan a trip to Alaska to study brownies. How will you get there? What will you take? Who will go with you? What will you see? Write a story about your trip.

Visit a zoo to see bears. How are brown bears similar to other kinds of bears and how are they different?

Glossary

biologist—a scientist who studies living things

carcasses—the bodies of dead animals

cubs—baby brown bears

den—a hidden, safe place where a brown bear spends the winter

habitat—an area where a kind of animal can live and grow

hibernates (HYE-bur-nates)—sleeps deeply. When a bear hibernates, its body slows down to help it survive the winter.

home range—an area in which an animal travels as it looks for food

litter—a group of baby bears born together

omnivores (AHM-nih-vorz)—animals who eat both plants and animals

predators (PREH-duh-turz)—animals who hunt other animals for food

sanctuary—a safe place

Index